The Most A
Joke Book

THE MOST AWFUL
by
Mary Danby
illustrated by
Bryan Reading
JOKE BOOK EVER

AAAGH!

An Armada Original

The Most Awful Joke Book Ever was first published
in the U.K. in Armada in 1984
This impression 1988

Armada is an imprint of
the Children's Division, part of
the Collins Publishing Group,
8 Grafton Street, London W1X 3LA

Printed and bound in Great Britain by
William Collins Sons & Co. Ltd, Glasgow

Jest for Fun

PATIENT: Oh, Doctor, I don't know what's the matter with me lately. Half the time I don't know where I am.
DENTIST: Open wide, please.

If you keep watching Mickey Mouse films, what's up with you?
You're having Disney spells.

"I won a prize at school today, Mummy," said little Becky. "Miss Trubshaw asked how many legs a hippopotamus has got, and I said, 'Three'."

"Three?" asked her mother. "Then how on earth did you win a prize?"

"I was closest," said Becky.

BARRY: What's five Q and five Q?
JAMES: Ten Q.
BARRY: You're welcome!

Why can't sharks learn French?
Because they know no "merci".

Did you hear about the wooden car with the wooden engine and wooden wheels?
   It wooden go.

Where do ghosts like to swim?
Lake Erie.

Roger took his dog to the vet and asked it there was anything that could be done to stop the dog wagging its tail.

"Whatever for?" asked the vet.

"Well, you see," explained Roger, "my headmaster is coming to our house this evening, and I don't want anything to suggest he's welcome."

SUNDAY SCHOOL TEACHER: Phyllis, why should we pray for grace?

PHYLLIS: Is it because she's such a naughty girl, miss?

What should you do if your nose goes on strike?
Picket!

WHO LOST A HERD OF ELEPHANTS?

BIG BO PEEP

POLICE CONSTABLE: I've brought in the suspect, Sarge.
SERGEANT: Has he got a record?
CONSTABLE: Yes, Sarge. Several, in fact. The latest Michael Jackson and a whole pile of Elvis Presleys.

Little Ernie bought an ice lolly in the school tuckshop. Before he could finish it, the bell went. Not wanting to waste the lolly, he put it in his trouser pocket.

The next lesson was geography.

"What do you call people who live in Africa?" asked the teacher.

"Africans," said a little girl.

"And what about people who live in Asia?"

"Asians," replied another.

"Now, Ernie," said the teacher. "Can you tell me what we call people who live in Europe?"

"Er . . . no," admitted Ernie.

"European!" shouted a voice from the back.

"No I'm not!" said Ernie indignantly. "My ice lolly's melting!"

HOW DO YOU CUT A BRONTOSAURUS IN HALF? WITH A DINO-SAW

9

TINA: Why didn't the spookess win the beauty contest?
MINA: Because she wasn't boo-tiful enough?
TINA: Yes, I'm afraid she didn't have the ghost of a chance.

What is a cannibal's favourite TV programme?
Man Alive.

An old lady went into an ironmonger's and bought a large quantity of steel wool.

"Are you planning to clean something very big?" asked the ironmonger.

"No," said the old lady. "I'm going to knit myself a car."

HARRY: What are you going to be when you grow up.
GARY: I'd like to be a policeman and follow in my father's footsteps.
HARRY: I didn't know your father was a policeman.
GARY: He isn't — he's a burglar.

If your father could see you now, he'd turn in his gravy

What clothes do barristers wear in court?
Lawsuits.

SON: How much pocket money can I have?
FATHER: Fifty pence a week.
SON: Fifty pence a week? That's an insult!
FATHER: O.K., I'll pay you monthly, then you won't be insulted so often.

Tommy's father rushed out of the bathroom waving his shaving brush. "This thing's useless!" he complained. "I can't shave with it."

"That's funny," said Tommy. "It was fine this morning when I washed my bike with it."

WHERE DO PIGS SLEEP?

IN HAMMOCKS

Dopey Dick wanted to start a chicken farm, and his friend gave him twenty chickens. After a few weeks, Dopey Dick went back to his friend to tell him all the chickens were dead. The friend kindly gave him twenty more.

Two months passed, and the friend went to visit him.

"Where are the chickens?" he asked, not seeing any around. "Don't tell me the second lot died, too."

"'Fraid so," said Dopey Dick. "You know, I think I may have been planting them too deep."

BOY IN CHEMIST'S: What would you do if someone stole a bottle of perfume?
CHEMIST: I'd put a detective on the scent.

CUSTOMER: Some rat poison, please.

SHOP ASSISTANT: I'm afraid we don't sell it. Have you tried Boots?

CUSTOMER: I want to poison them, not to kick them to death.

Every summer, old Miss Blenkinsop asked her greengrocer to pack up a box of plums and send it to the Queen at Buckingham Palace.

One year, the greengrocer said: "Excuse me, but why do you always send plums to the Queen?"

"Because it tells you to in the National Anthem," explained Miss Blenkinsop. "Where it says 'Send her Victorias'."

How did the people of Paris find Quasimodo?
They followed a hunch.

PATIENT: Doctor! Doctor! I feel like a car.
DOCTOR: Well, park yourself over there.

A man lost his ear in an accident at work and asked his friend to help him look for it. After a while, his friend found his ear. "That's not mine," said the man, "mine had a pencil behind it."

MOTHER: Don't you know that reaching over the table for cakes is bad manners? Haven't you got a tongue?
MATTHEW: Yes, but my arms are longer.

Last night, a stationery shop was broken into and a number of blunt pencils were stolen. The police describe the theft as pointless.

WHAT DO YOU CALL A COWBOY WITH PAPER TROUSERS?

A RUSTLER

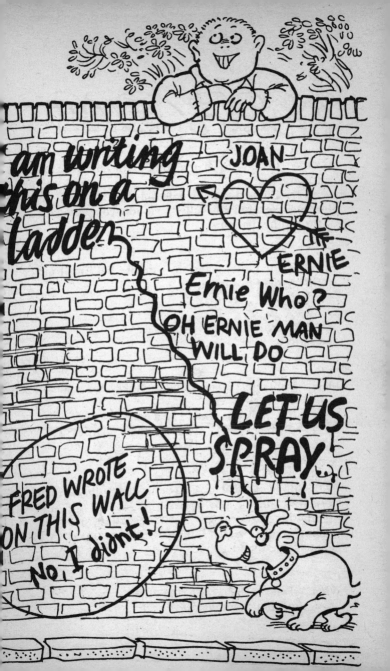

GOOFY GAGS

DENTIST: I'll have to charge you £40 for removing that tooth.
PATIENT: But you said it would only be £10.
DENTIST: Yes, but you yelled so loudly you scared off three other patients.

I'd tell you the story about the window, but I'm afraid you'd see right through it.

What do werewolves call a fur coat?
"Darling".

BILL: I can't make up my mind whether to be a poet or a painter.
BEN: Oh, I think you should be a poet.
BILL: You mean you've read one of my poems?
BEN: No, I've seen one of your paintings.

At the top of an escalator in a department store, Alan stood watching the moving handrail.
   "Anything wrong, young man?" asked a shopper.
   "No," replied Alan. "I'm just waiting for my chewing gum to come round again."

What did one volcano say to the other?
"Now don't blow your top, dear."

JILL: We had duck for lunch, and our cat ate the left-overs.

JANE: Then he must have been a duck-filled fattypuss!

Robert was travelling by himself in a hot air balloon. As he passed a farm, he called down to the farmer: "Hallo there! Where am I?"

The farmer looked up. "You can't fool me," he shouted. "You're up there in that little basket!"

Why was the thief caught stealing a trayful of watches?
Because he took too much time.

MIMI: Did you hear about the parrot that laid square eggs? It could only say one word.

FIFI: What was that?

MIMI: Ouch!

WHAT DO FRENCHMEN EAT FOR BREAKFAST?

HUIT HEURES BIX

A man saw a farmer leading a beautiful horse along the road.

"Excuse me," he said, "but if that horse is for sale I'd like to offer you a thousand pounds for her."

"Well now," replied the farmer, "she doesn't look too good."

"Nonsense," said the man. "She looks quite all right to me. One thousand five hundred."

"Oh, I don't think so." The farmer shook his head. "Anyway, she's not for sale."

"Two thousand," persisted the man. "My final offer."

"As I said," answered the farmer, "she doesn't look too good, but if you want her that much, have her."

Later that day the man arrived at the farmhouse looking furious. "You cheat!" he shouted at the farmer. "You sold me a blind horse!"

"There you are," said the farmer. "I told you she didn't look too good."

The geography teacher was telling her class about Scotland. "Who can tell me," she said, "what Scots mean by 'lads and lasses'?"

"I know," said Phyllis. "Lads are boys and Lassies are dogs."

ERIC: My rich uncle fell off a cliff last week.
DEREK: Were you very close?
ERIC: Just close enough to push him.

What two words have the most letters?
Post Office.

MOTHER: Did the butcher have pigs' trotters, Jane?
JANE: I couldn't see, Mum. He had his shoes on.

MARTIN: When I was in China, I saw a woman hanging from a tree.

LYNN: Shanghai?

MARTIN: Not very. About four feet off the ground.

A party of schoolboys were going to France on a cross-channel ferry.

"Now then," said the headmaster, "let's check on safety drill. What do you do if a boy falls overboard?"

"Shout 'boy overboard!', sir," said Michael.

"Correct. And what if a teacher falls overboard?"

"Er — which one, sir?"

PATIENT: Doctor, doctor, I feel like an apple.

DOCTOR: Cor!

"I've had a letter from your teacher, Gavin," said his father. "He says you're very careless about your appearance."

"Really, Dad?"

"Yes. You haven't appeared in school for three weeks."

Why are opticians so agreeable?
Because they always see eye to eye with their customers.

POLICEMAN: I'm afraid I'll have to lock you up.
BAD BERT: What's the charge?
POLICEMAN: No charge — it's all part of the service.

Why don't vampires get kissed much?
Because they have bat breath.

st TEACHER: Very boring television last night.
nd TEACHER: Did you watch it?
st TEACHER: No.
nd TEACHER: Then how do you know it was boring?
st TEACHER: I had lots of homework from 4C!

A man fell off some scaffolding and was taken to hospital. After being X-rayed, he was told by a doctor: "You've broken your arm in three places."

"You're wrong there," the man replied. "I was in the same place all morning."

In the fight between a hedgehog and a squirrel, who won?
The hedgehog won on points.

ELLA: My teacher brought a maths plant to school today.
BELLA: How do you mean?
ELLA: She said it had square roots.

Why did the tonsils get dressed up?
Because the doctor was taking them out.

"How old are you now, Darren," asked his auntie.
"How do you mean?" answered Darren. "When I'm on a bus, when I go to the cinema, or in real life?"

PASSER-BY: Why is the level crossing gate half open?
RAILMAN: Well, we're half expecting a train.

Did you hear about the werewolves' party? It was a howling success.

GEOGRAPHY TEACHER: If you were in mid-Atlantic, facing South, what would be on your right hand?
SMART ALEC: Four fingers and a thumb.

The Teddy Bear went to work on a building site. While he was having his tea break, someone stole his pickaxe. He complained to the foreman.

"But didn't you know?" said the foreman. "Today's the day the Teddy Bears have their picks nicked!"

PATIENT: "Doctor, everyone thinks I'm cricket-crazy."
DOCTOR: "How's that?"
PATIENT: "Oh, no! Not you as well!"

I once tried writing a new National Anthem. But it was no good. Nobody would stand for it.

WHY DOES A TAP DRIP?

BECAUSE IT CAN'T SNIFF

29

Dennis came home from school. "Guess what, Dad," he said. "I've got some great news for you."

His father looked pleased. "What's that, Dennis?"

"Well, you remember you promised me £5 if I passed my exams?"

"Yes," said his father eagerly.

"You'll be glad to hear I've spared you the expense."

FARMER: I crossed a cow with a kangaroo.
VISITOR: What did you get?
FARMER: I'm not sure, but you have to milk it on a pogo stick.

A little girl wrote an essay entitled "Home Cooking".

"When roasting lamb," she began, "my mother puts her leg in the oven."

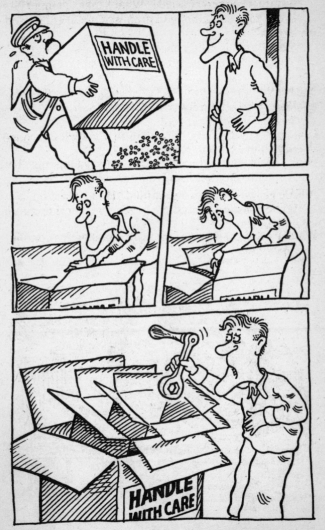

31

TEACHER: Give me a sentence starting with I, Nicholas.
NICHOLAS: Yes, sir. I is —
TEACHER: No, no, Nicholas! You don't say "I is", you say "I am".
NICHOLAS: All right, sir. I am the ninth letter of the alphabet.

Why should New York's sky be clearer than London's?
Because New York has more skyscrapers.

Advertisement in a newspaper:
LOST: Black and white dog with half its tail missing. Torn ear. Blind in one eye. Limps a bit. Answers to the name of Lucky.

What do you get if you cross an elephant with a computer?
A four-ton know-all.

PATIENT: Doctor, I keep stealing chairs.
DOCTOR: That's all right. Take a seat.

What happened to the man with two wooden legs whose trousers caught fire?
He was burnt to the ground.

TEACHER: What's twelve times twelve?
SARAH: A hundred and forty-four.
TEACHER: Good, Sarah.
SARAH: Good, miss? It's perfect!

What is the scariest fairy tale?
Ghouldilocks and the Three Brrrs.

Well, the sign says "TIP THE WAITRESS"

Jim and Jeff went off on their bikes for a picnic in the woods. They had one bottle of lemonade between them. Jim went to explore while Jeff unpacked the food. When he returned, he found the bottle was empty.

"Hey!" he exclaimed crossly. "Half of that was mine!"

"I know," said Jeff, "but I was thirsty, and as my half was at the bottom of the bottle I had to drink through yours to get to it."

ROTTEN RIDDLES

Which American state has the most werewolves?
Hairizona.

What is Rupert Bear's middle name?
the

What is eight foot tall, green and wrinkled?
The Incredible Hulk's granny.

What do you get if you cross a zebra with a whale?
A traffic jam.

What do sheikhs use to hide from their enemies?
Camelflage.

What do you get if you eat Christmas decorations?
Tinsel-itis.

How do you feel after you're bitten by a vampire?
Holier.

Why can't two elephants go swimming at the same time?
Because they've only got one pair of trunks.

Which cowboy actor is always broke?
Skint Eastwood.

Why did they give the postman the sack?
To put his letters in.

How many people have lived in Wales?
Only one - Jonah.

What do librarians wear?
Book jackets.

What is the nearest thing to Silver? The Lone Ranger's bottom.

Why are Londoners stupid?
Because the population there is so dense.

What do you get if you cross a cow and a tortoise?
Longlife milk.

What do you get if you cross a bee and a polecat?
Something that stings and stinks at the same time.

How do you make a monster stew?
Keep it waiting for a couple of hours.

What is a comedian's favourite motor bike?
A Yama-ha-ha!

What is black and white and has eight wheels?
A nun on roller skates.

What do you call the small rivers that run into the Nile?
Juveniles.

How do you make anti-freeze?
Hide her nightie.

How do you make a bandstand?
Take all the chairs away.

Where do you get trees from?
The tree shop. They have branches everywhere.

What do you call a reluctant rooster?
A cock-a-doodle-don't.

What happened to the boy who missed the school bus?
He caught it when he got home.

Why is it unwise to buy a cheap violin?
Because it might be a fiddle.

How do Eskimos dress?
As quickly as possible.

Why should you always carry a clock in the desert?
Because it has a spring in it.

What comes after Humphrey?
Humphour.

Who was the first Avon lady?
Mrs. Shakespeare.

Who did not invent the aeroplane?
The Wrong Brothers.

What's big, hairy and can fly?
King Kongcorde.

What do you get if you cross a chicken and a bell?
An alarm cluck.

What is the best place for a party on board ship?
Where the funnel be.

Where is Felixstowe?
At the end of his foot.

Why does a barber never shave a man with a wooden leg?
Because he always uses a razor.

What's chocolate outside, peanut inside, and sings
hymns?
A Sunday School Treet.

How do you stop a cold going to your chest?
Tie a knot in your neck.

What happened to the lady who washed her front
doorstep?
She broke her washing machine.

If mud makes bricks and bricks makes walls, what do walls
make?
Ice-cream.

43

What is bright red and silly?
A blood clot.

Why did the man call his dog Sandwich?
Because he was half-bred.

What do monsters put on their roast beef?
Grave-y.

Where do Londoners with spots live?
'Ackney.

What did the mummy broom say to the baby broom?
"Go to sweep."

Corny Cackles

During school dinner, the teacher asked: "Any complaints?"

"Yes," said David. "The peas are hard as rocks."

The teacher reached over with his fork and picked up some peas from David's plate. "They seem soft enough to me," he said, tasting them.

"Well, they would be," said David. "I've been chewing them for the last ten minutes!"

BILL: Ugh! I just ate an apple with a worm in it.
JILL: Here, have some water to wash it down.
BILL: Nah, let him walk down!

What has bread on both sides and is cowardly?
A chicken sandwich.

Ali Baba stood outside the cave entrance and commanded: "Open Sesame!"

From inside the cave, a voice replied: "Open says-a-who?"

TEACHER: How far is it to Pakistan?
CHARLIE: Well, it can't be too far. My friend Tariq comes from Pakistan, and he goes home for his dinner every day.

News Item:
Several dirty saucepans have been stolen. The police are scouring the countryside.

A man stepped on some scales that announced: "Learn Your Fate, Your Weight and Your Fortune." He put some money in a slot and received a printed card.

"You are amazingly clever and hard-working," it said. "Everything you touch turns to gold."

His wife took the card from him, read it and said: "It's got your weight wrong, too."

PATIENT: Doctor! Doctor! I've a pain in my lower back.
DOCTOR: We must get to the bottom of this.

What does a disc jockey suffer from?
Spins and needles.

TEACHER: Who said "I come to bury Caesar, not to praise him"?
LIZZIE: The undertaker?

What do little zombies play with?
Deady Bears.

46

FATHER: How many times have I told you to stop playing
    with that calculator?
SON: Er . . . 343,128.2.

Two astronauts arrived at the Pearly Gates. St. Peter said:
"If you'll just wait a moment I'll check your files and see if
I can let you in."

"Actually, we don't want to come in," said one of the
astronauts.

"Really?" said St. Peter. "Then what *do* you want."

"Please sir," said the second astronaut, "can we have
our satellite back?".

LUCY: Mummy, you know that walking, talking, crying
    doll you bought me?
MUMMY: Yes, dear.
LUCY: Well, it's just been sick!

WHAT DO RED INDIANS PUT ON THEMSELVES AFTER A BATH?

SCALP'EM POWDER

JIMMY: Mum, the kids at school call me Bighead.
MOTHER: Don't worry, son, there's nothing in it.

What did Dracula say to his bride?
"Hi, gore-juice!"

HOSPITAL DOCTOR: Well, Mr. Peabody, I have some
 good news and some bad news for you. Which would
 you like first?
MR. PEABODY: The bad, please.
DOCTOR: Well, the bad news is that we have to amputate
 both your feet.
MR. PEABODY: And the good news?
DOCTOR: The man in the next bed wants to buy your
 slippers.

For her bithday, Molly was given a beautiful charm
bracelet. She wore it to school, but nobody seemed to
notice it. Eventually she stood up and said: "Isn't it hot in
here! I think I'll take off my bracelet."

"Excuse me," said the man on the doorstep to the lady of the house, "but I pass this way every day and I've seen you through the window hitting your little boy on the head with a loaf of bread."

"So?" said the lady.

"This morning you didn't hit him with a loaf of bread — you hit him with a chocolate gateau."

"Well," the lady replied, "today's his birthday."

PATIENT: Doctor, I feel like fumes coming out of a car.
DOCTOR: Now, now, you mustn't exhaust yourself.

What happens to liars after death?
They lie still.

51

CUSTOMER: Waiter, there's no chicken in this chicken pie.
WAITER: So? You don't get dog in a dog biscuit, either.

What has four legs but only one foot?
A bed.

VAMPIRE VICTIM: May I have a glass of water please?
VAMPIRE: Why, are you thirsty?
VAMPIRE VICTIM: No, I want to see if my neck leaks.

What is worse than a redskin on the warpath?
A banana skin on the footpath.

SUNDAY SCHOOL TEACHER: Who sits at the right hand of
   God?
PUPIL: Er — Mrs. God?

FRANK: Why did you call both your sons Edward?
JIM: Because two Eds are better than one.

A candidate in a local election called at a house, and the door was opened by a little girl.

"Is your mummy in the Conservative Party or the Labour Party?" asked the candidate.

"Neither," said the little girl. "She's in the lavvy."

What is the best thing to do when you are hungry?
Nothing . . . you will soon get fed up.

FATHER: Well, Sylvia, did you get the best marks in your class this term?
SYLVIA: No, Daddy. Did you get the best salary in your office?

What is rhubarb?
Bloodshot celery.

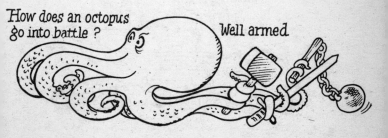

How does an octopus go into battle?

Well armed

1st COMIC: I have to get a potato clock.
2nd COMIC: A potato clock? Why?
1st COMIC: I have to get a potato clock so I can be at work
by nine o'clock.

What do you call a Russian who's just run a marathon?
A red sweater.

1st SPIRITUALIST: My mother is a medium.
2nd SPIRITUALIST: Is she really? Mine is a large.

Two men were in a compartment on a train. One of them
got up and opened the window. The other one closed it.
The first one opened it. The second one closed it again.

"Hey," said the first man, "what do you think you're
playing at?"

"Draughts," replied the other man. "Your move, isn't
it?"

PATIENT: Doctor! Doctor! I think I'm a lift.
DOCTOR: You look all right to me.
PATIENT: But I feel I'm coming down with something.

A man was buying a Rolls-Royce and wanted to pay cash, but he found he was 2p short of the £15,000 needed. Outside the car showrooms he saw a man selling newspapers, and he went out and asked him:

"Could you lend me 2p? I want to buy a Rolls-Royce."

"Sure," replied the man. "But look — here's 4p. Buy one for me as well."

Why couldn't the car play football?
Because it had only one boot.

What's that revolting ugly thing on your neck?
Oh, sorry, it's your head!

TER: And now for my next song . . . What shall it be?
ESTER: Do you know "Loch Lomond"?
TER: Of course I do.
ESTER: Then kindly go and jump in it.

at do misers do in cold weather?
around a candle.

at do misers do in very cold weather?
ht it.

TIENT: Doctor, doctor, I think I'm invisible.
CTOR: Who said that?

new a man who was so unpopular that his phone didn't
g even when he was in the bath.

57

RIBTICKLERS

PATIENT: Doctor, can you give me something for wind?
DOCTOR: Certainly. Here's a kite.

Mr. and Mrs. Perkins were driving through an Afric
game park when they saw a baby antelope.

"Stop the car!" said Mrs. Perkins. "I want to see if I c
get close to it."

But no sooner had she left the car than a lion leapt o
from behind a bush and began to carry her off.

"Shoot!" she shrieked to her husband. "For Pete's sak
shoot!"

"I can't!" he shouted back. "I've run out of film!"

TEACHER: Where are rhinos generally found?
SUSIE: Please, miss, rhinos are so large they hardly ev
get lost.

Why shouldn't you pull a tiger by his tail?
It may only be his tail, but it could be your end.

ROSE: How was your trip to the U.S.A.?
LILY: Fine, but when my husband saw the Grand Canyo
his face fell a mile.
ROSE: Was he disappointed with the view?
LILY: No, he fell over the edge.

What did the prisoner say when he knew he was going to be tortured to death on the rack?
"Oh dear, it looks as if I'm in for a long stretch."

CK: My brother is very unusual. He does farmyard impressions.
CK: What's unusual about that?
CK: He doesn't do the sounds, he does the smells . . .

Have you heard about the man who slept with his head under the pillow?
He woke in the morning to find that the fairies had taken all his teeth.

Why is the sky so high?
So the birds don't bump their heads.

GEORGE: What sound does a Scottish car make?
ANGUS: It hoots, mon.

KEVIN: Dad, can you write in the dark?
DAD: Sure I can. What do you want me to write?
KEVIN: Your name on my report card.

Why did Dopey Dan drive into the sea?
Because he was told to dip his headlights.

PATIENT: Doctor! Doctor! I keep thinking I'm a bird.
DOCTOR: Perch there and I'll tweet you in a minute.

What's the difference between a stupid person and a welsh
rabbit?
One is easy to cheat and the other is cheesy to eat.

What did the Koala take on holiday?

Just the bear essentials

DRIVING INSTRUCTOR: Slow down please.

LEARNER: I'm only doing 25 miles an hour. You're allowed to do 30 in this area.

DRIVING INSTRUCTOR: Yes, but not on the pavement.

How did the chimpanzee escape from his cage?
With a monkey wrench.

LARRY: Can you telephone from a space ship?

LARRY: Of course I can tell a phone from a space ship!

What's a Hindu?
It lays iggs.

SUE: I want to buy a small mirror.
SHOP ASSISTANT: A hand mirror, miss?
SUE: No. One for seeing my face in.

Where do dressmakers live?
On the outskirts of a city.

PATIENT: Doctor, I feel like a mountain.
DOCTOR: Don't worry — we'll soon have you in peak
   condition"

How do zoo animals greet each other?
"Hi, Ena!" and "'Ello, Phant!"

TEACHER: Who was the first woman?
LINDA: I don't know.
TEACHER: Of course you do. She had something to do
   with an apple.
LINDA: I know. Granny Smith!

1st GHOST: Nobody seems to notice us any more.
2nd GHOST: No, we might as well be dead for all they care.

How can you tell a miser's house?
By the tea-bags on the washing line.

A group of tourists were visiting an ancient battlefield.
   "See that rock," said their guide. "That's where King Harold fell."
   "I'm not surprised," said a tourist. "I nearly tripped over it myself."

PATIENT: I feel strange. I think I can see into the future.
DOCTOR: When did this start?
PATIENT: Next Tuesday.

Why do elephants drink so much water?
Because they don't like beer.

PATIENT: Doctor, how am I?
DOCTOR: Just fine. You'll live to be ninety.
PATIENT: But I *am* ninety.
DOCTOR: There, what did I tell you?

Did you hear about the couple who lived in a lighthouse?
Their marriage was said to be on the rocks.

Two eggs were in a saucepan, and one said: "Phew! Hot in
here, isn't it!"
  "Yes," said the other one, "but just wait till you get out
— you'll get your head smashed in!"

A week before his birthday, Mrs. Jones bought her son Matthew a new bicycle and hid it in the shed. "Now Jenny," she said to his sister, "don't go telling Matthew about his present."

The next day, Matthew said to his mother: "I like the new bike, Mum!"

Mrs. Jones was furious with Jenny. "I thought I told you not to tell him," she said,

"I didn't," said Jenny. I showed him."

Where do laundresses usually hang out?
On clothes lines, of course.

SUNDAY SCHOOL TEACHER: Why did Mary and Joseph take little Jesus to Jerusalem with them?
EMILY: Was it because they couldn't get a baby-sitter?

When's the best time to play golf?

at tee time

1st MONSTER: Do zombies like the dead?
2nd MONSTER: Of corpse they do!

What is a shark's favourite hobby?
Anything it can sink its teeth into.

Little Sally, in her first year at primary school, told her mother that she had broken off her engagement to her classmate Bobby Smith.

"Oh dear," said her mother. "What happened?"

"Well," replied Sally, "I decided he just isn't ready for marriage yet. And besides, he scribbled in my colouring book."

MOTHER: You'll burst if you eat any more.
DANNY: Well pass me another slice of cake — then stand back!

WHY WAS CINDERELLA A ROTTEN FOOTBALLER?

BECAUSE SHE HAD A PUMPKIN FOR A COACH

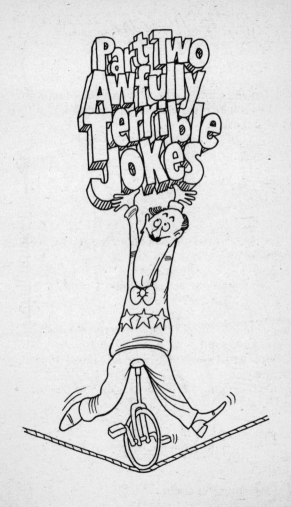

Part Two Awfully Terrible Jokes

nutty cracks

FRED: Do you wake your wife with a cup of tea?
BILL: Yes. I take it to her in my pyjamas.
FRED: That's nice.
BILL: Yes, but my pyjamas get a bit soggy.

How does a robot stand?
Bolt upright.

LES: Last week I was thrown out of the zoo for feeding the monkeys.
DES: What's so bad about that?
LES: I was feeding them to the lions.

Jimmy went into the pet shop.
"Can I have some budgie seed?" he asked.
"I didn't know you had a budgie," said the man behind the counter.
"I haven't," Jimmy replied, "I want to grow one."

TEACHER: What was the Charge of the Light Brigade?
SALLY: Was it a bill from the Electricity Board, miss?

How does a monster count to 33?
On his fingers.

MILLIE: I wish I had been born a hundred years ago.
MOTHER: Good gracious! Why?
MILLIE: Well, you wouldn't dare tell a little old lady to make her own bed.

A woman told her husband what she wanted for her birthday. "Something with plenty of diamonds in it, please."
    Her wish was granted. He gave her a pack of cards.

MOTHER: Why are you home from school so early?
TOMMY: I was the only one who could answer a question.
MOTHER: Oh! Really? What was the question?
TOMMY: Who threw a pencil at the headmaster?

What has a bottom at the top?
A leg.

72

DAUGHTER: Daddy, Daddy — Mum's going out!
FATHER: Well pour some more paraffin on her, then.

What do vegetarian cannibals eat?
Swedes.

"Hands up all those who want to go to Heaven," said the Sunday School teacher.

Everyone put their hands up except Kenneth.

"Don't you want to go to Heaven, Kenneth?"

"I can't, miss," said Kenneth. "My mum told me to come straight home."

What did the German say to the broken clock?
"Ve haff vays off makink you tock!"

Why don't doctors feel queasy on boats?

Because they're accustomed to see sickness

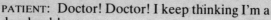

PATIENT: Doctor! Doctor! I keep thinking I'm a doorknob!
DOCTOR: All right, all right! Don't fly off the handle . . .

Fred went swimming in the sea, and when he came out all his clothes were gone. What did he go home in? Why, the dark, of course.

How many letters are there in the alphabet?
Twenty-four. There used to be twenty-six, but E.T. went home.

JOHN: My dad raises chickens.
RON: Really? Mine raises hell.

Why couldn't the car play football?
Because it had only one boot.

What do you get if you cross a parrot and an elephant?
Something that tells everything it remembers.

PETER: I wish I'd lived a long time ago.
TEACHER: Why?
PETER: Then I'd have less history to learn.

A boy wanted to have his name up in lights, so he changed his name to Exit.

What makes the Tower of Pisa lean?
It doesn't eat much.

JUDGE: You have been found guilty of murdering your mother and father. Before I pass sentence, is there anything you wish to say?

PRISONER: Yes. I should like it taken into consideration that I'm an orphan.

Two little bees were pestering their father. Eventually he said: "Either beehive yourselves — or buzz off!"

Why does Batman carry worms?
To feed Robin.

FRED: Is that the book your dad wrote on boxing?
NED: Yes, he calls it his scrapbook.

TEACHER: Who wrote *King Solomon's Mines?*
ALICE: Old King Cole?

"Mum, now that I'm fifteen, can I wear eye-shadow and lipstick and mascara and perfume and wear high heels?"
    "No, Sidney, you may not."

MANDY: What shall I do? It says here I've got to write an essay on an elephant.
ANDY: What you need is a ladder, then.

Ricky brought his friend home to play. "Can Donkey stay for tea?" he asked his mother.
    "Why do you call him Donkey?" she asked.
    The other boy answered: "Oh, eeyore, eeyore — 'e always call me that."

BOY: Did you ever see anyone like me before?
GIRL: Yes, once. But I had to pay admission.

What do you call a Scottish parrot?
A Macaw.

PATIENT: Doctor! Doctor! I'm at death's door!
DOCTOR: Don't worry — I'll pull you through.

Did you hear about Fat Fred? He was so big that when he needed a shower he had to go for a car wash.

LITTLE BOY: How old are you, Mummy?
MOTHER: I'm 40.
LITTLE BOY: Gosh, you don't look it.
MOTHER (pleased): Really?
LITTLE BOY: No, but I expect you did once.

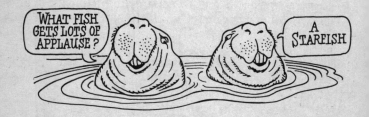

Why did the pilot crash into the house?
Because the landing lights were on.

VICAR: Now, children. What do we know about Good
  Friday?
ALICE: Was he the one who looked after Robinson
  Crusoe?

The condemned murderer waited in his cell. The day of
execution had arrived. At 8 a.m. the prison governor, two
warders and a priest came to the cell.

"Before we take you to your place of execution," said
the governor, "do you have any last request?"

"Yes," answered the prisoner. "I'd like to sing a song."

"Go ahead, then," said the governor.

The man began to sing: "One hundred million billion
green bottles, hanging on the wall . . ."

FRED: My grandfather won't live much longer. You might
  say he's got one foot in the grate.
NED: Don't you mean the grave?
FRED: No, he wants to be cremated.

Why did the tide turn?
Because the seaweed.

What do you call a nutter with a car on his head?
Jack.

What do you call a nutter with shovel, sitting at the bottom of a hole?
Doug.

And what do you call a nutter with a shovel, sitting at the bottom of a smaller hole?
Douglas.

JENNY: My mother's an angel.
PENNY: Really?
JENNY: Yes, she's always harping on about something.

What happened to the boy who ate a window?
He had a pane in his stomach.

CUSTOMER: Remember that hair restorer you sold me?
BARBER: Certainly I do, sir. Would you like another
bottle?
CUSTOMER: Er, no. You see, my wife thought it was
furniture polish, and, well — could you come and shave
our sideboard?

What's a cannibal's favourite game?
Swallow the leader.

DOCTOR: How's the broken rib?
PATIENT: Well, I keep getting a stitch in my side.
DOCTOR: Fine — that shows the bones are knitting.

What time is it when a cake is divided between four
people?
A quarter to four.

TEACHER: Didn't you read the notice? It says "No Running Allowed".

MAGGIE: Yes, but I was running quietly.

What's the difference btween a drink of tea and a magician?

One's a cuppa and the other's a sorcerer.

SMITH: "Do you suppose a giraffe gets a sore throat if he gets his feet wet?"

JONES: "Yes — but not until the next week."

What tools do we use in arithmetic?

Multipliers.

DOCTOR: Those pills I gave you to help you remember things — how are they working?

PATIENT: What pills?

WHAT DRINK DO JUNGLE CATS PREFER?

LYONS QUICK BREW

What is the saddest piece of clothing?
Blue jeans.

FRED: "Why are you holding up that slice of bread?"
NED: "I'd like to propose a toast!"

Where does a ghoul keep his hands?
In a hand bag.

SUNDAY SCHOOL TEACHER: Where was Solomon's
    temple?
BILLY: On the side of his head.

How many successful jumps does a skydiver have to make before he can join the Skydivers' Association?
All of them.

TEACHER: Use the word ANTENNAE in a sentence.
CHARLIE: O.K. There antennae chips left.

Why is it useless to send a telegram to Washington?
Because he is dead.

A man took his son to a restaurant, and both ordered steak.

The boy heard his father say to the waiter, "Well done."

"Why are you praising the waiter?" he asked. "He hasn't even brought the steaks yet."

WHAT DO YOU CALL A FLYING POLICEMAN?　　A HELICOPPER

STEVE: "We never wanted for anything when I was a kid."

CAROL: "I'm glad to hear it."

STEVE: "Except for my brother Alf, that is. He was wanted for burglary."

What did Hamlet say as he entered the slimming clinic?
"Tubby or not tubby, fat is the question!"

What's the difference between a farmer and a dressmaker?
One gathers what he sows and the other sews what she gathers.

ELSIE: My doctor told me to take three of these pills on an empty stomach.

MABEL: Did they work?

ELSIE: I don't know. They kept rolling off in the night.

How do you find out where a flea has bitten you?
You start from scratch.

A man took his pet to Cruft's Dog Show. One of the officials came up to him and said:

"Excuse me, but that's a very unusual breed you have there. What is it?"

"It's a long-nosed, long-tailed terrier," replied the man. "Mind you," he added, "some people call them alligators."

TEACHER: Angie, if your father earned £500 a week and gave your mother half, what would she have?"

ANGIE: Heart failure.

Who looked after Finderella?
Her Fairy Codmother.

Why did the man jump from the top of the Empire State Building?
Because he wanted to make a hit on Broadway.

TERRY: My dad's a professional fighter. A featherweight.
GERRY: Light, is he?
TERRY: No, he tickles his opponents to death.

Were Elijah's parents rich or poor?
Rich, because they made a good prophet.

EDDIE: Why does your new baby cry so much, Mrs Green?
MRS GREEN: Well, if you had no hair, and all your teeth were out, and your legs were so weak you couldn't stand on them, you'd probably cry yourself.

Psychiatrists are so busy nowadays that some of them have double decker couches.

What do you get if you leave bones in the sun?

A SKELETAN

PATIENT: Doctor! Doctor! I keep thinking I'm a tennis racket.
DOCTOR: Don't worry, I expect you're highly strung.

Where do fish wash?
In a river basin.

TEACHER: If you get ducks in cricket and fowls in football, what do you get in bowls?
WAYNE: Porridge, sir.

Do robots have brothers?
No, only transistors.

JUDGE: Why do you only burgle third-floor flats?
PRISONER: Well, Your Honour, that's my storey and I'm
    sticking to it.

What did the inventor of carpets make?
A pile.

CUSTOMER: Have you got Jane Austen's *Pride and
    Prejudice?*
BOOKSHOP ASSISTANT: I don't know — when did she
    order it?

What kind of lights did Noah have on the ark?
Floodlights.

DOTTY DAYS

What do you call a female goat?
A buttress.

PATIENT: Doctor, I think I'm a fruitcake.
PSYCHIATRIST: What's got into you?
PATIENT: Oh, flour, nuts, raisins — all the usual
ingredients.

When is the cheapest time to telephone your friends?
When they're out.

POLICEMAN: Your dog keeps chasing a man on a bicycle.
MAN: Nonsense, Officer. My dog can't ride a bicycle.

Where is Timbuktu?
Between Timbuk-one and Timbuk-three.

1st COMIC: My wife takes me to the pub in her car.
2nd COMIC: Really?
1st COMIC: Yes — she drives me to drink.

Who sings in your ear?
Wax Bygraves.

CUSTOMER: Waiter, there's a hair in this honey.
WAITER: It must have come from the comb, sir.

How do you annoy a shop assistant?
Go into a second-hand shop and ask: "What's new?"

PATIENT: Doctor! Doctor! I feel like an ice-cream.
DOCTOR: So do I, go and buy me one.

What is the difference between a kangaroo and an Egyptian mummy?
One bounds around; the other is bound around.

TEACHER: What is a Fjord?
JOHNNY: A Scandinavian motor car.

Why was the dog sent out of the flea circus?

Because he stole the show!

What happened to Lot's wife?
When she turned round she was a-salted.

What will a lion eat in a restaurant?
The waiter!

Who owns all the milk in Saudi Arabia?
A milk sheik.

If a flea and a fly pass each other, what time is it?
Fly past flea.

What is richer, a bay or a river?
A river. It has two banks.

What do you call a baby whale that cries?

A little blubber

ABEL: How do you like the new doctor?

MABEL: Oh, he's ever so sympathetic. He makes you feel really ill.

Hear about the man who kept racing pigeons?
The pigeons always won.

BILL: Did you hear what happened when Gordon sent his picture to the Lonely Hearts Club?

PHIL: No, what?

BILL: They sent it back. They said they weren't that lonely . . .

What do Eskimos use for money?
Ice lolly.

WHICH CRICKET TEAM PLAYS IN ITS UNDERWEAR?

THE VEST UNDIES

MOTHER: Aunt Edna won't kiss you with that dirty face.
JOHNNY: That's just what I figured.

What's a big-game hunter?
Someone who loses his way to a football match.

PATIENT: Doctor! Doctor! You must help me. I think I'm
a month of the year.
DOCTOR: Then MARCH over here, JUNE, and I MAY
have a look at you.

What do you call fake spaghetti?
Mock-aroni.

My dog loves classical music. All he says is Bach, Bach,
Bach . . .

Why do monsters forget so easily?
Because everything goes in one ear and out the others.

PATIENT: Doctor! Doctor! I'm becoming invisible.
DOCTOR: Yes, I can see you're not all there.

What do Red Indians shout at Bingo?
Wigwam!

TEACHER: How do you spell "banana"?
EMMA: I know how to start but I don't know when to stop.

What do jelly-babies wear?
Gumboots.

WHAT DO YOU GET IF YOU CROSS A PINCUSHION WITH A SKUNK?

A PORCUPONG

Punny Ones

How should a ghost-hunter keep fit?
He must exorcise regularly.

Why did the man trip over the shrimp?
Beacuse he was accident prawn.

What exam must debtors take?
Their owe levels.

Why did the antelope?
Nobody gnu.

What was the German barber called?
Herr Cutt.

How do we know that Moses wore a wig?
Because he was sometimes seen with Aaron and sometimes not.

Why is Wales such a damp place?
Because there are so many leeks in it.

What happened when Honor met Lulu?
They ran Hawaii together.

What do musical Indians play?
Haydn Sikh.

Why is a woodcutter like an actor?
Because he's always taking boughs.

Why would nobody visit the ghost?
Because he had such a ghastly manor.

What's black and wet and hairy?
A North Sea Oil wig.

WHAT'S SMALL GREEN AND DOES GOOD DEEDS?

A BOY SPROUT

OU: Do sailors go on overland expeditions?
UCY: Not safaris I know.

Why do fish hate Coca-Cola?
Because it's the reel thing.

What happened when the cows became tangled with the milking machine?
There was udder chaos.

FRANKENSTEIN'S MONSTER: I want a ghoul friend!
ARON FRANKENSTEIN: O.K. I'll see what I can dig up.

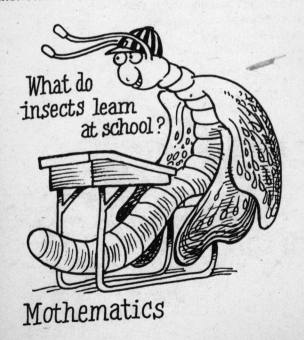

What do insects learn at school?

Mothematics

What was the first mention of a walking stick in the Bible?
When Eve presented Adam with a little Cain.

1st ACTOR; I was once in a play called *Breakfast in Bed*.
2nd ACTOR: Did you have a big rôle?
1st ACTOR: No, just toast and marmalade.

What was Dr. Jekyll's favourite game?
Hyde and Shriek.

SAM: I feel absolutely whacked!
BEN: Tired?
SAM: No, the headmaster just caned me.

What's the best way to count cows?
On a cow-culator.

What do ghosts eat for breakfast?
Deaded wheat.

How do frogs cross the road?
They follow the green cross toad.

Why did the psychiatrist put his wife under the bed?
Because he thought she was a little potty.

How do boys and girls laugh?
"He, he, he!" and "Her, her, her!"

What is a snake's favourite opera?

Wriggletto

What do you get if you cross Dracula with a hot dog?
A fangfurter.

Where can you go to get satisfaction?
A satisfactory.

What gravedigger is a famous singer?
Bury Many-Low.

JACKIE: What's this bridge we're crossing?
FATHER: It's the Forth Bridge.
JACKIE: Funny, I could swear it was only the third.

Once, the Ancient Britons wore nothing but woad. Then they put Anglo sacks on.

What is the dreariest pudding?

Apple grumble

my karate teacher is ill
I think he's got kung flu

Who was the skinniest emperor?
Napoleon Boneypart.

What building has the most storeys?
A library.

Why did the cowboy jump off the coach?
Because he got stage fright.

Where do ghouls go to church?
Westmonster Abbey.

What vegetable plays snooker?
A cue-cumber.

TEACHER: Kindly don't hum while you're working.
GAVIN: I'm not working — just humming!

What do you get if you cross a centipede with a chicken?
Fewer fights over who gets the drumsticks.

PATIENT: Doctor! Doctor! I keep thinking I'm a comedian!
DOCTOR: You must be joking!

Where do spiders play football?
Webley.

ANNIE: Did I tell you the joke about the rope?
FANNY: No.
ANNIE: Oh, let's skip it.

"Dear Problem Page,
   "I've been going out with my boyfriend for six weeks, and I've just found out he has a wooden leg. Should I break it off?"

What's the best thing to eat in the bath?
Sponge cake.

PATIENT: Doctor! Doctor! I feel like a needle!
DOCTOR: Yes, I see your point.

If the stork brings human babies, who brings giant babies?
Cranes.

ZOO OWNER: Is it difficult to bury a dead elephant?
VET: Yes, it's a huge undertaking.

What is always in front of you and yet you can't see it?
Your future.

HE: Do you play the piano by ear?
SHE: No, I prefer to use my hands.

What is a caterpillar? A worm in a fur coat

Why can't you play cards on a ship?
Because the captain will keep standing on the deck.

PATIENT: Doctor, all I can think of is gin, gin, gin!
DOCTOR: What you need is a tonic.

What is the best cure for water on the knee?
Drainpipe trousers.

A scientist has successfully crossed a hyena with a talking parrot. Now he knows what hyenas laugh at.

MOTHER: Eat up your liver.
GINNY: But it's tough.
MOTHER: I expect that's because it's full of iron.

113

WAITER: How would you like your coffee, sir?
CUSTOMER: Without.
WAITER: Without what?
CUSTOMER: Without your thumb in it.

Why do bears have fur coats?
Because they'd look stupid in anoraks.

Why is it hard to keep a secret at the North Pole?
Because you can't stop your teeth chattering.

How do you keep a monster from smelling?
Cut off his nose.

Dopey Dick bought a zebra. What did he call it?
Spot.

TOURIST: That cow over there — such a pretty colour.
FARMER: A Jersey, that is.
TOURIST: *Really*? I thought it was its skin.

For the Policeman's Supper tonight, there will be beetroot soup. The Chief Superintendent is investigating the cream, while constables are pounding the beet.

116

What's the difference between a kangaroo and a lumberjack?
One hops and chews, the other chops and hews.

JIMMY: On the school bus today a little boy fell off his seat, and everyone laughed except me.
MOTHER: Well done. Who was the little boy?
JIMMY: Me.

The chambermaid knocked on the door of the hotel bedroom.

"Come in!" said a voice.

She opened the door and saw a man lying in bed.

"Good morning!" she said. "Are you the gentleman who wanted to be woken in time to catch the early train?"

"Yes," replied the man.

"Well you can go back to sleep again," she told him. "You've missed it!"

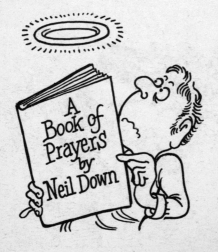

"Good afternoon, Mrs. Smith," said the doctor. "And what can I do for you?"

"It's my husband," said Mrs. Smith. "I'm afraid he's broken his wooden leg. Could you let him have another?"

The doctor obliged, but a few days later she returned, with the same request. The doctor gave her another wooden leg, and told her to ask her husband to be more careful. However, she was back the following week, and again the week after.

Very suspicious by now, the doctor asked her: "What on earth has your husband been doing? That's four new legs he's had."

At this point, Mrs. Smith broke down and confessed. "The truth is, doctor," she said, "he's making a coffee table."

What do you call a London Underground train full of geniuses?
A tube of Smarties.

What do cats eat for breakfast?
Mice Krispies.

Dopey Dick bought a new washbasin.
   "Would you like a plug for it?" asked the shopkeeper.
   "Oh, said Dopey Dick, "I didn't know it was electric."

How does a bird land in an emergency?
By sparrow 'chute.

TEACHER: Why are you always late for school, Keith?
KEITH: Because you always ring the bell before I get here.

Which man ran the fastest in the 100 metres?
The winner.

Why was Baron Frankenstein never lonely?
Because he was good at making friends.

HUSBAND: Why can't you make bread like my mother?
WIFE: I would, if you could make dough like your father!

A headless man went to a Lost Property desk.
The clerk looked at him and said: "Sorry, love, can't help you. You need our Head Office."

TEACHER: Louis, use these words in a sentence —
defence, detail, deduct, defeat.
LOUIS: De-feat of de-duct went over de-fence before de-tail.

What do you get if you cross a private eye with loud music and flashing lights?
A disco tec.

When does a potato wear spectacles?

When it's a Spectator

Where does a Red Indian ghost sleep?
In a creepy teepee.

A labourer came home one day to his lodgings and found his landlady trying to change a light bulb above the dining-room table.

"Here," he said, "let me help you." He clambered on to the table in his wet and muddy boots.

"I'll get some newspaper for you to stand on," said the landlady, eyeing his footprints on the table.

"Oh, it's O.K., thanks," he replied. "I can reach."

What does the Invisible Man call his mother and father?
His transparents.

Why don't elephants drink martinis?
You wouldn't either if the olives got stuck up your nose!

A man walked into a pub and asked the barman: "Do you serve Scotsmen?"

"Certainly, sir," replied the barman.

"Good," said the man. "I'd like a pint of beer for me, and two Scotsmen for my crocodile."

DENTIST: Stop yelling! I haven't touched your tooth yet.
BARRY: I know, but you're standing on my foot!

Why did the chicken run on to the football pitch?
Because the referee blew for a fowl.

Can you bear any more?

THE AWFUL JOKE BOOK

compiled by Mary Danby

Here is another brain-boggling collection of
ghastly gags, hideous howlers, riotous riddles
and witty wisecracks — illustrated with scores
of hilarious cartoons.
You'll drive your family and friends
round the bend!

What is the main ingredient in dog biscuits?
Collie flour.

NEW COWHAND: What is the name of this ranch?
RANCHER: The Lazy G Triple Diamond Circle S
    Bar Z.
NEW COWHAND: How many head of cattle are there?
RANCHER: Not many. Only a few of them survive the
    branding.

Armada

THE WHIZZKID'S HANDBOOKS

1, 2 & 3

Peter Eldin

Is the strain of school giving you brain failure? Don't despair — there *is* a cure!

These hilarious Handbooks will tell you all you need to know to become your Class Whizzkid and always Come Out On Top. Each book is packed with jokes, puzzles, brainteasers and tricks — plus a delicious bunch of devilish devices to make and stunts to pull. There are lots of hints and tips, too, to help you baffle your teachers with your brilliance.

TOP SECRET
ADULTS
KEEP OUT!

Armada

Armadas are chosen first by children all over the world. They're pocket-sized and pocket money-sized — and they make terrific presents for friends. They're colourful and exciting and there are hundreds of titles to chose from — baffling mysteries, daring adventures, spine-chilling horror stories, rib-tickling joke books, thrilling stories about schools and ponies — and lots more. Armada has something for everyone.